S0-BAS-835

BOYNTON BEACH CITY LIBRARY

JUN 2 5 2018

LIVING WITH DISEASES AND DISORDERS
Diabetes and Other Endocrine Disorders

LIVING WITH DISEASES AND DISORDERS

Diabetes and Other Endocrine Disorders

REBECCA SHERMAN

SERIES ADVISOR

HEATHER L. PELLETIER, Ph.D.

Pediatric Psychologist, Hasbro Children's Hospital
Clinical Assistant Professor, Warren Alpert Medical School of Brown University

MASON CREST

Mason Crest
450 Parkway Drive, Suite D
Broomall, PA 19008
www.masoncrest.com

© 2018 by Mason Crest, an imprint of National Highlights, Inc. All rights reserved. No part of this publication may be reproduced or transmitted in any form or by any means, electronic or mechanical, including photocopying, recording, taping, or any information storage and retrieval system, without permission from the publisher.

MTM Publishing, Inc.
435 West 23rd Street, #8C
New York, NY 10011
www.mtmpublishing.com

President: Valerie Tomaselli
Vice President, Book Development: Hilary Poole
Designer: Annemarie Redmond
Copyeditor: Peter Jaskowiak
Editorial Assistant: Leigh Eron

Series ISBN: 978-1-4222-3747-2
Hardback ISBN: 978-1-4222-3756-4
E-Book ISBN: 978-1-4222-8037-9

Library of Congress Cataloging-in-Publication Data
Names: Sherman, Rebecca, author.
Title: Diabetes and other endocrine disorders / by Rebecca Sherman; series consultant:
  Heather Pelletier, PhD, Hasbro Children's Hospital, Alpert Medical School/Brown University.
Description: Broomall, PA: Mason Crest, [2018] | Series: Living with diseases and disorders |
  Includes index.
Identifiers: LCCN 2016053113 (print) | LCCN 2016053887 (ebook) | ISBN 9781422237564
  (hardback: alk. paper) | ISBN 9781422280379 (ebook)
Subjects: LCSH: Diabetes—Juvenile literature. | Endocrinological disorders
Classification: LCC RC660.5 .S54 2018 (print) | LCC RC660.5 (ebook) | DDC 616.4/62—dc23
LC record available at https://lccn.loc.gov/2016053113

Printed and bound in the United States of America.

First printing
9 8 7 6 5 4 3 2 1

QR CODES AND LINKS TO THIRD PARTY CONTENT
You may gain access to certain third party content ("Third Party Sites") by scanning and using the QR Codes that appear in this publication (the "QR Codes"). We do not operate or control in any respect any information, products or services on such Third Party Sites linked to by us via the QR Codes included in this publication and we assume no responsibility for any materials you may access using the QR Codes. Your use of the QR Codes may be subject to terms, limitations, or restrictions set forth in the applicable terms of use or otherwise established by the owners of the Third Party Sites. Our linking to such Third Party Sites via the QR Codes does not imply an endorsement or sponsorship of such Third Party Sites, or the information, products or services offered on or through the Third Party Sites, nor does it imply an endorsement or sponsorship of this publication by the owners of such Third Party Sites.

TABLE OF CONTENTS

Key Icons to Look for:

Words to Understand: These words with their easy-to-understand definitions will increase the reader's understanding of the text, while building vocabulary skills.

Sidebars: This boxed material within the main text allows readers to build knowledge, gain insights, explore possibilities, and broaden their perspectives by weaving together additional information to provide realistic and holistic perspectives.

Educational Videos: Readers can view videos by scanning our QR codes, which will provide them with additional educational content to supplement the text. Examples include news coverage, moments in history, speeches, iconic sports moments, and much more.

Text-Dependent Questions: These questions send the reader back to the text for more careful attention to the evidence presented there.

Research Projects: Readers are pointed toward areas of further inquiry connected to each chapter. Suggestions are provided for projects that encourage deeper research and analysis.

Series Glossary of Key Terms: This back-of-the-book glossary contains terminology used throughout the series. Words found here increase the reader's ability to read and comprehend higher-level books and articles in this field.

SERIES INTRODUCTION

According to the Chronic Disease Center at the Centers for Disease Control and Prevention, over 100 million Americans suffer from a chronic illness or medical condition. In other words, they have a health problem that lasts three months or more, affects their ability to perform normal activities, and requires frequent medical care and/or hospitalizations. Epidemiological studies suggest that between 15 and 18 million of those with chronic illness or medical conditions are children and adolescents. That's roughly one out of every four children in the United States.

These young people must exert more time and energy to complete the tasks their peers do with minimal thought. For example, kids with Crohn's disease, ulcerative colitis, or other digestive issues have to plan meals and snacks carefully, to make sure they are not eating food that could irritate their stomachs or cause pain and discomfort. People with cerebral palsy, muscular dystrophy, or other physical limitations associated with a medical condition may need help getting dressed, using the bathroom, or joining an activity in gym class. Those with cystic fibrosis, asthma, or epilepsy may have to avoid certain activities or environments altogether. ADHD and other behavior disorders require the individual to work harder to sustain the level of attention and focus necessary to keep up in school.

Living with a chronic illness or medical condition is not easy. Identifying a diagnosis and adjusting to the initial shock is only the beginning of a long journey. Medications, follow-up appointments and procedures, missed school or work, adjusting to treatment regimens, coping with uncertainty, and readjusting expectations are all hurdles one has to overcome in learning how to live one's best life. Naturally, feelings of sadness or anxiety may set in while learning how to make it all work. This is especially true for young people, who may reach a point in their medical journey when they have to rethink some of their original goals and life plans to better match their health reality.

Chances are, you know people who live this reality on a regular basis. It is important to remember that those affected by chronic illness are family members, neighbors, friends, or maybe even our own doctors. They are likely navigating the demands of the day a little differently, as they balance the specific accommodations necessary to manage their illness. But they have the same desire to be productive and included as those who are fortunate not to have a chronic illness.

This set provides valuable information about the most common childhood chronic illnesses, in language that is engaging and easy for students to grasp. Each chapter highlights important vocabulary words and offers text-dependent questions to help assess comprehension. Meanwhile, educational videos (available by scanning QR codes) and research projects help connect the text to the outside world.

Our mission with this set is twofold. First, the volumes provide a go-to source for information about chronic illness for young people who are living with particular conditions. Each volume in this set strives to provide reliable medical information and practical advice for living day-to-day with various challenges. Second, we hope these volumes will also help kids without chronic illness better understand and appreciate how people with health challenges live. After all, if one in four young people is managing a health condition, it's safe to assume that the majority of our youth already know someone with a chronic illness, whether they realize it or not.

With the growing presence of social media, bullying is easier than ever before. It's vital that young people take a moment to stop and think about how they are more similar to kids with health challenges than they are different. Poor understanding and low tolerance for individual differences are often the platforms for bullying and noninclusive behavior, both in person and online. Living with Diseases and Disorders strives to close the gap of misunderstanding.

The ultimate solution to the bullying problem is surely an increase in empathy. We hope these books will help readers better understand and appreciate not only the daily struggles of people living with chronic conditions, but their triumphs as well.

—Heather Pelletier, Ph.D.
Hasbro Children's Hospital
Warren Alpert Medical School of Brown University

WORDS TO UNDERSTAND

acute: severe symptoms or disease that happen quickly or for a short time.

autoimmune: type of disorder where the body's immune system attacks the body's tissues instead of germs.

cell metabolism: chemical reactions that take place inside cells to turn food into energy.

chronic: symptoms or disease that are ongoing, lasting a long time.

complications: a damaging condition or illness that occurs as a result of an injury or disease.

endocrine system: the collective term for the glands that produce hormones in the human body.

glands: organs in the body that produce substances such as hormones.

glucose: a simple sugar molecule that serves as a primary energy source for most living creatures.

hormones: substances the body produces to instruct cells and tissues to perform certain actions.

insulin: a hormone produced in the pancreas that controls cells' ability to absorb glucose.

mutation: a change in the structure of a gene; some mutations are harmless, but others may cause disease.

progressive disease: a disease that generally gets worse as time goes on.

CHAPTER ONE

What Is the Endocrine System?

You have probably heard of diabetes. More than 29 million Americans have it—almost 1 out of every 10. You almost certainly know someone with diabetes. Maybe that person is a grandparent or an elderly neighbor. It is very common among older adults, but kids can get it, too. If you have diabetes, you're not alone—more than 200,000 people in the United States under the age of 20 have diabetes. But what is diabetes?

Diabetes is not just one illness. It's the name given to a number of diseases that share some of the same symptoms. Some of these diseases are rare, while others are extremely common. All the different forms of diabetes affect the **endocrine system**. The endocrine system is made up of **glands** that produce **hormones**. Hormones are a kind of language the body uses to communicate with its cells and tissues. They are signals that tell cells what to do, and how fast to do it. Some hormones tell the body to grow. Others tell the body how to use the energy it gets from food. Hormones can control moods, sleep cycles, and many other things. When a body has trouble making certain hormones

More than 200,000 American kids and teens have diabetes.

or understanding their instructions, cells and tissues may not work the right way. This can cause very serious illness—how serious depends on the hormone involved and what that hormone controls.

The Endocrine System

These are some of the major glands of the endocrine system, along with some of the hormones they produce:

- **Hypothalamus.** This gland is a kind of control center for the endocrine system. It produces several hormones that direct other glands to produce hormones. It is located in the brain.
- **Pituitary gland.** Just under the hypothalamus at the base of the brain, the pituitary gland produces growth hormone, vasopressin, and many other hormones that control the production of hormones in the thyroid, adrenal, and ovaries or testes.
- **Thyroid.** Located in the neck, this gland produces thyroid hormone, which controls the speed of your metabolism.
- **Adrenal glands.** These are two glands located on top of your kidneys. Their outer layer (the adrenal cortex) produces cortisol and aldosterone, which are important to many body processes. The inner part of the adrenal glands produces adrenaline.
- **Pancreas.** This organ has two completely different functions. Most of the pancreas isn't part of the endocrine system at all—it produces enzymes

EDUCATIONAL VIDEO

Scan this code for a video about the endocrine system.

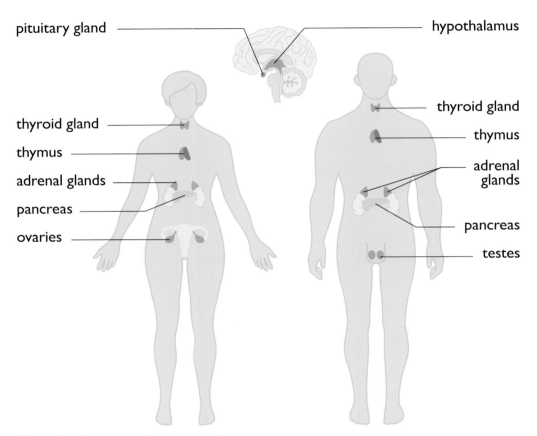

The endocrine system in women and men.

to help with digestion. But it also contains small clumps of cells called the islets of Langerhans, after the person who first discovered them in a microscope. The islets of Langerhans produce several different hormones, including insulin, glucagon, and somatostatin. These three work in concert to regulate how much glucose your cells use.

- **Ovaries/testes.** Also known as the gonads, these produce sex hormones. The ovaries produce estrogen and progesterone, while the testes produce testosterone.

Diabetes Mellitus

Diabetes is divided into two major categories. The most common kind, diabetes mellitus, is a **chronic** illness. That means it is a lifelong condition and has no known cure. It occurs when the body has trouble making or responding to a hormone called **insulin**. Insulin helps control **cell metabolism**, the process by which cells make energy. Insulin allows cells to make energy using **glucose**, a kind of sugar.

A healthy person digests glucose from food. Glucose is absorbed into the bloodstream, which transfers it all over the body for cells to use. But if the body doesn't make enough insulin or can't properly use insulin, glucose builds up in the bloodstream. When blood glucose levels get high, the body begins sending excess glucose to the kidneys. The kidneys filter toxins from the blood and send them to the bladder in urine. Someone with very high blood sugar will have to urinate a lot, because the body is trying to get rid of excess glucose.

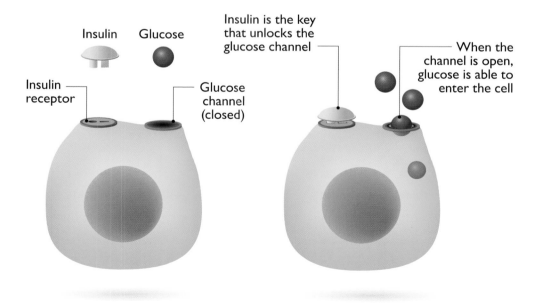

Insulin helps the body regulate glucose levels.

CELL METABOLISM

To make a car go, you fill it with gasoline and turn it on. The engine mixes tiny drops of gasoline with air, and ignites the mixture. The energy created by these small explosions turns the wheels of the car.

The cells of your body get energy in a comparable process. Instead of gasoline, cells mix glucose with oxygen. This combination creates chemical energy in the form of a molecule called ATP, for adenosine triphosphate.

To get gasoline into your car, you have to open the little door that protects the gas cap. That door is locked and must be opened with either a key or by flipping a switch inside the car. Then you can pump gasoline into the fuel tank of your car.

Cells are enclosed by a cell wall. To get glucose into a cell, you have to use insulin to unlock an entrance in that wall. If there's no insulin, or if the insulin isn't working, it's like cells have lost the key to the gas tank. Even if they're at the gas station, they can't pump fuel in the car.

Diabetes mellitus can cause many types of **complications**. **Acute** complications can occur suddenly at any time during the course of the disease. Chronic complications develop over a long time, often several years. Both the acute and the chronic complications of diabetes mellitus can be very serious, even life-threatening. People with diabetes mellitus must learn to carefully manage their blood sugar levels in order to reduce their risk of developing complications. Depending on what type of diabetes they have, they may need daily injections of insulin. They may take medications. They have to monitor their diet, especially their intake of sugars and nutrients that break down into sugar.

Types of Diabetes Mellitus

- *Type 1 diabetes.* An **autoimmune** disease that occurs when the body's immune system attacks and destroys the cells that produce insulin. People with type 1 diabetes are insulin-dependent. They need a daily supply of injectable insulin.
- *Type 2 diabetes.* The body produces insulin, but cells have trouble using it. People with type 2 diabetes develop what is called insulin resistance. This is a **progressive disease**—it gets worse over time if not treated adequately. People with type 2 diabetes may eventually become insulin-dependent.
- *Gestational diabetes.* Like type 2 diabetes, gestational diabetes involves insulin resistance. It occurs in pregnant women, and it goes away once the baby is born. Women who have had gestational diabetes are at greater risk for developing type 2 diabetes later in life. Their children are also at greater risk for type 2 diabetes.
- *Monogenic diabetes.* A single **mutation** in any one of several different genes can cause diabetes. These mutations are quite rare, accounting for 1–2 percent of all diabetes cases. Some mutations result in diabetes that can be treated with medication. Others lead to insulin dependency. The mutations generally run in families. Collectively they are known as MODY, or maturity-onset diabetes of the young.

Diabetes Insipidus

Diabetes insipidus is the second category of diabetes. It is rare, affecting 1 in every 30,000 children. It is also a chronic disease, although it can develop temporarily for short periods of time following certain types of surgery. People with diabetes insipidus have trouble either making or processing a hormone that helps regulate the amount of water in the body. This hormone, called

Pregnant women are vulnerable to gestational diabetes. Fortunately, it usually goes away after the baby is born.

vasopressin, signals to the kidneys how much urine to send to the bladder. Most people with diabetes insipidus don't make enough of this hormone, and their kidneys send too much water to the bladder. Medication can correct this problem easily.

A very small percentage of people with diabetes insipidus have enough vasopressin, but their kidneys fail to respond to the hormone correctly. People with this condition, called nephrogenic diabetes insipidus, need to carefully manage how much water they drink and the levels of salt in their diet.

Other Kinds of Endocrinological Disease

Two different glands can cause diabetes insipidus: the adrenal gland or the pituitary gland. It's not the only endocrinological disorder that has more than one cause. For example, some kids show signs of puberty very early. Others have very delayed puberty. Both early and late puberty can be caused by hormonal problems, but which hormones? And which glands?

The pituitary gland, the adrenal glands, and the reproductive organs all produce hormones involved in puberty. Doctors have to determine which gland and hormone is out of whack before deciding how to treat early or late puberty. Often no treatment is required. But, if it is necessary, medication can supply the missing hormone, or limit an overabundant one.

Diseases of the Adrenal Glands

- *Addison's disease.* Caused by either an autoimmune disease or by a genetic disorder, Addison's disease occurs when the adrenal glands do not produce enough cortisol, a multipurpose hormone. It is treated with medication to supply the missing hormones.
- *Congenital adrenal hyperplasia (CAH).* A genetic disease in which the adrenal glands do not make cortisol, but instead make too much

androgen, a hormone that controls the development of sexual organs and characteristics. Kids with CAH may show signs of puberty very early. Rarely, CAH can keep a person from producing enough mineralocorticoids, hormones that control how much salt is in the body. Treatment usually involves medication to replace the missing hormones.

Diseases of the Thyroid Gland

- *Graves' disease.* An autoimmune disease in which the immune system attacks the thyroid gland, causing it to increase the amount of thyroid hormone produced. Thyroid hormone regulates the speed at which the body uses energy. Too much makes the body use energy more quickly, a condition called hyperthyroidism. Treatment may involve medication, surgical removal of the thyroid, or the administration of radioactive iodine, which disables the thyroid gland over the course of a couple of months. After treatment, people may need to take medication to supply thyroid hormone.

THE DOCTOR DRANK WHAT?

Diabetes comes from an ancient Greek word meaning "to flow through." That's a polite way of saying "to urinate a lot." *Mellitus* means sweet or honeyed. *Insipidus* means tasteless. Diabetes mellitus and diabetes insipidus distinguish between "sweet" urine and "tasteless" urine. Yuck!

For most of human history, physicians had very few tools with which to diagnose disease. They made do with the evidence they could gather using their own five senses—including their sense of taste.

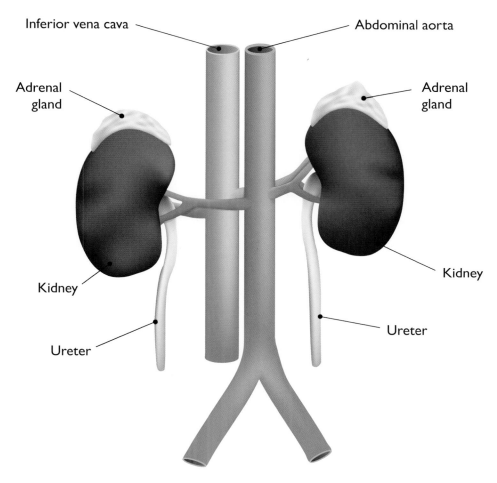

Inferior vena cava

Abdominal aorta

Adrenal gland

Adrenal gland

Kidney

Kidney

Ureter

Ureter

The adrenal glands sit on top of the kidneys.

- *Hashimoto's disease.* An autoimmune disease in which the body attacks the thyroid gland, reducing the amount of thyroid hormone produced and causing the body to use energy more slowly. This is called hypothyroidism. Hypothyroidism is treated with daily medication to replace the missing thyroid hormone.

Two men with gigantism stand next to a more typically sized man in Kashmir (undated photo).

Diseases of the Pituitary Gland

- *Gigantism.* A very rare disease in which the pituitary gland produces too much growth hormone. This usually happens because a benign (noncancerous) tumor has formed on the pituitary. Someone with gigantism may grow very large compared to other people that age.
- *Growth hormone deficiency.* When the pituitary gland does not make enough growth hormone, children may grow more slowly, or not at all. Someone with a growth hormone deficiency may be unusually small for his or her age. Treatment may involve medication to supply more growth hormone.

Text-Dependent Questions

1. What are hormones?
2. A shortage of what hormone causes diabetes mellitus? What role does that hormone play in the body?
3. What hormone regulates how quickly the body uses energy? What gland produces that hormone? Name two diseases caused by problems with that hormone.

Research Projects

Look at the interactive diagram of the endocrine system at KidsHealth. org (https://secure02.kidshealth.org/kid/htbw/_bfs_ESactivity.html). How many of the glands can you label? Click on the solution if you get stuck.

WORDS TO UNDERSTAND

autoantibodies: instead of fighting germs, these antibodies attack the body's own tissues, causing autoimmune disease.

cannula: a tiny tube inserted into the body for administering medicine.

dehydration: when the body doesn't contain enough water to function properly.

diabetic ketoacidosis: a life-threatening condition caused when hyperglycemia, ketosis, and dehydration combine.

hyperglycemia: high blood sugar (too much glucose in the bloodstream).

hypoglycemia: low blood sugar (not enough glucose in the bloodstream).

ketosis: a dangerous condition in which the bloodstream contains too many ketone bodies, which are produced when cells burn fats for energy.

lancet: a tiny surgical knife with a sharp point used to collect a drop of blood for glucose testing.

syringe: a device that uses pressure to inject liquid into the body through a hollow needle.

CHAPTER TWO

Type 1 Diabetes and Insulin Dependence

If you have type 1 diabetes, you have to plan every step of your day—eating, being active, even sleeping. It's hard work, and you never get a day off. It can be exhausting. Sometimes, you may get mad about your diabetes. If so, it helps if you can talk to someone who understands what you're going through.

You might be surprised how many people do know exactly what you're going through: 1.25 million. That's how many Americans live with type 1 diabetes. Another 40,000 people are diagnosed with it every year. The most common ages to be diagnosed are either between the ages of five and seven, or right around puberty. That's why type 1 diabetes used to be known as "juvenile diabetes."

For reasons that scientists don't yet understand, the percentage of people in the population with type 1 diabetes has been rising since the start of the 21st century. If current trends continue, researchers predict that three times as many young people will have type 1 diabetes by 2050 as did in 2000. That's the bad news. The good news is that people with diabetes have more tools than ever before for managing their disease.

Kids with type I diabetes often need help keeping track of their glucose levels.

One hundred years ago, diabetes was a death sentence. Very few people lived more than a few months after falling ill with it. Now a kid with type 1 diabetes can expect to live not just to adulthood, but well into old age. Taking good care of yourself is the key to a healthy life with type 1 diabetes.

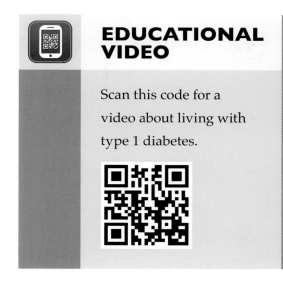

EDUCATIONAL VIDEO

Scan this code for a video about living with type 1 diabetes.

Autoimmune Attack

No one knows why type 1 diabetes develops. But we do know how it happens. It has nothing to do with how much sugar you ate, or anything else you did. It has to do with your immune system. The body's immune system produces cells designed to attack germs that might harm the body. But sometimes immune cells begin attacking the body's own tissues. These malfunctioning immune cells are called **autoantibodies**. In type 1 diabetes, people develop autoantibodies that attack cells in a part of the pancreas called the islets of Langerhans.

There are several different kinds of cells in the islets of Langerhans, and each produces a different hormone. Type 1 diabetes begins when autoantibodies attack beta cells, which produce insulin. The more beta cells get destroyed, the less insulin the body can make. With less insulin, the body has a harder and harder time using glucose from food. Glucose remains in the bloodstream and builds up to high levels, a condition called **hyperglycemia**. A person experiencing hyperglycemia may feel unusually thirsty and exhausted. He or she may have to urinate a lot. Weight loss, constant hunger, and blurry vision are other common symptoms.

As the autoimmune attack continues to destroy beta cells, insulin levels plummet. Cells that cannot get glucose begin burning fats for energy. That releases

DIABETIC DOGS AND DISCOVERY

Frederick Banting

In 1889, two scientists in Germany, Oskar Minkowski and Josef von Mering, performed an experiment in which they surgically removed a dog's pancreas. That dog developed diabetes, proving that the disease and the pancreas were linked. But how?

In 1921, a young doctor in Toronto named Frederick Banting discovered the answer. Banting and a research assistant named Charles Best surgically removed the pancreases of two dogs. As with the earlier experiment, the dogs developed diabetes. This time, Banting and Best took the removed pancreases and made an extract solely from the islets of Langerhans. They injected that extract into one of the dogs, who recovered; the other dog died in a few days.

They repeated the test on several more dogs, using extracts derived from cows. Again the dogs that received the extracts survived. The excited researchers, now including John MacLeod and Bertram Collip, developed ways to purify this extract, which they named "insulin." First given to a patient in 1922, it was hailed as a miracle drug for its ability to revive diabetic children on the brink of death.

acids called *ketone bodies* into the bloodstream. If too many ketones build up in the bloodstream, a person develops **ketosis**, and suddenly gets very sick. Symptoms may include fruity-smelling breath, stomach pain, nausea, and vomiting.

Ketosis can be mistaken for a very bad stomach bug. Without proper treatment, ketosis will combine with hyperglycemia and loss of body fluid (**dehydration**) to cause **diabetic ketoacidosis** (DKA). This is an extremely dangerous condition that may lead to a coma, or even death. Nearly 30 percent of children with type 1 diabetes are hospitalized for DKA at the time of their diagnosis. Scientists hope that, in the future, screening for autoantibodies to beta cells may allow developing cases of type 1 diabetes to be diagnosed and treated long before people get so dangerously sick.

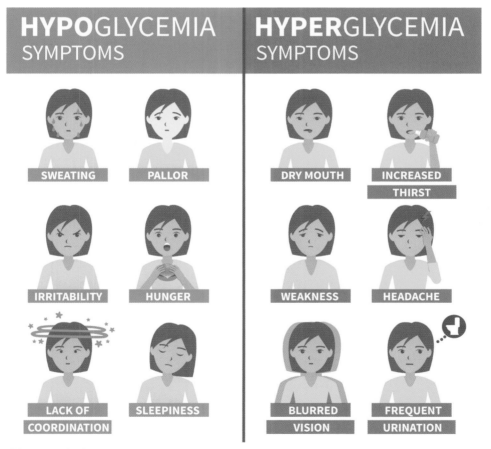

Problems with glucose levels can cause hyperglycemia (discussed here) or hypoglycemia (discussed on page 32).

Insulin Dependence

Right now, doctors don't know of any way to stop or reverse the autoimmune attack on beta cells once it begins. Under constant siege by autoantibodies, beta cells never get a chance to recover. Eventually, they are all destroyed, and the body cannot make insulin at all. In order to survive, people with diabetes must have an outside source of insulin available. Insulin can't be taken by mouth because it is destroyed by stomach acids. It must be injected.

Some people inject insulin with a small **syringe**, or with a device containing a syringe, like an injection pen. There are many different insulin medications. Some are long-acting, and are given once per day. Intermediate-acting insulin covers about half a day, or overnight. Short-acting insulin takes effect about 30–60 minutes after it's given and is often used before meals. Rapid-acting insulin takes effect right away.

How much insulin any given person needs depends on a lot of different factors, which may change from one day to the next. Two injections per day is

Some insulin injectors look like a pen.

FROM DEAD ANIMALS TO LIVING FACTORIES

Once scientists discovered that insulin treats diabetes, they had to figure out where to get it. The first medical insulin was made from the pancreases of animals being slaughtered for food. Cattle and pigs provided the vast majority of insulin, although there were exceptions. During World War II, one young diabetic refugee named Eva Saxl managed to make her own insulin medication from the pancreases of water buffalo. Originally from Czechoslovakia, she and her husband made enough water buffalo insulin for all of her fellow diabetic refugees in the Chinese city of Shanghai until the war ended.

Today, insulin available in the United States is synthetically produced. Yeast or bacteria is genetically engineered with human DNA, instructing it to make insulin. The insulin produced by these living factories is then harvested for medical use.

Pictured above: an advertisement for insulin made from animals.

generally the minimum, usually timed around meals. It is common to use more than one type of insulin. Someone who uses a long-acting insulin may also use short-acting or rapid-acting insulin at meals.

Other people with diabetes use an insulin pump. This device is the size of a cellphone that contains an insulin reservoir, a computer chip, a screen, and a battery. The pump clips to a person's clothing. Insulin flows from the pump through tubing to a small plastic tube called a **cannula**, which is inserted into the fatty tissue just below the skin and secured with a special kind of tape. The cannula has to be taken out and replaced every few days. The pump is programmed to deliver small doses of short-acting insulin throughout the day. This can free people with diabetes from having to inject themselves with a syringe multiple times per day. But someone with an insulin pump should always have an emergency supply of syringes and insulin, just in case the pump stops working.

Blood Glucose Monitors

Keeping tabs on your blood glucose levels is a key part of caring for yourself if you have type 1 diabetes. To do so, you need a working blood glucose monitor. There are many different kinds; many of them fit in a pocket. To use the monitor, you must first prick your finger with a small sharp device called a **lancet**. This causes your finger to bleed a little bit. You put the drop of blood on a little piece of special plastic called a test strip. The test strip is then inserted into the monitor. The monitor reads the blood on the strip and displays a number on its screen. This number represents the amount of glucose in your body, in milligrams per deciliter of blood. Your blood glucose is well controlled if this number is within a certain range. The range varies from person to person; your doctor will help you figure out the best range for you. Most people with type 1 diabetes need to check their blood glucose levels several times a day: after waking up in the morning, before a meal, and before or after exercise.

A continuous glucose monitor has a sensor, which is placed under the skin of your belly. It measures blood glucose levels every 1–10 minutes, and wirelessly transmits that information to the monitor. The monitor can be set to sound an

An insulin pump.

alarm if your blood glucose is too high or too low. Some continuous glucose monitors can work with certain insulin pumps to automatically adjust insulin depending on blood glucose levels. When a system like this works reliably, it takes a lot of the worry out of caring for diabetes. But it isn't perfect yet, and it is expensive. So some people choose the older method of monitoring instead.

Complications

There are two major reasons to do all this work of monitoring blood glucose levels. The first is to avoid the acute complications of diabetes. Hyperglycemia can happen if you eat too much, or if you miss a dose of your insulin. It may happen if you're not getting enough exercise, or if you're sick. We've already seen what can happen when someone gets hyperglycemic: ketosis and diabetic ketoacidosis. A similar dangerous condition caused by very high blood sugar levels is known as *hyperosmolar hyperglycemic state.*

THE SUPREMES

After insulin was discovered in 1922, one of the first patients to be treated with it was a wealthy American girl named Elizabeth Hughes. Her father, Charles Evans Hughes, had been on the Supreme Court before resigning to run for president, and he used his influence to get his daughter this new lifesaving medicine.

Forty years later, in a New York City housing project, a newly diagnosed seven-year-old girl learned to give herself her insulin shot. Blood glucose monitors didn't exist yet. She learned to tell if she was going high or low by paying close attention to how she felt. The determination that young Sonia Sotomayor used to face her diabetes has helped her achieve amazing goals throughout her life. In 2009 she became the third woman, and the first person of Puerto Rican heritage, to be appointed to the Supreme Court.

Photo above: Supreme Court Justice Sonja Sotomayor is congratulated by President Obama on her first day on the bench, in 2009.

There are also acute complications if someone's blood glucose levels get too low. This is called **hypoglycemia**, and it can happen if you miss a meal or snack, or if you take more insulin than you need. It can also happen if you've just gotten a lot of exercise, or if you're sick.

The symptoms of hypoglycemia include getting shaky or jittery and breaking out into a sweat. You might feel nervous or irritable, angry, or confused. A sudden change of behavior, an inability to concentrate, weakness, headache, and blurry vision are also possible symptoms of hypoglycemia. It is really important to test your blood glucose and eat something with glucose in it right away if you feel hypoglycemic. Untreated hypoglycemia can cause you to have seizures or lose consciousness. It can be life-threatening.

Someone with type 1 diabetes should always have access to a quick-working source of glucose in case hypoglycemia develops. Some people carry glucose tablets, small amounts of juice, or raisins. Your health-care team will help you and your family figure out what you should always have on hand in case of acute complications.

The other reason to monitor blood sugar levels is to avoid chronic complications. Studies show that keeping blood glucose within an acceptable range can significantly lower the risk of developing problems over a long period of time. Chronic complications are a major concern for people with any type of diabetes mellitus, whether or not they are insulin-dependent. We'll learn more about chronic complications in chapter 3.

Text-Dependent Questions

1. Explain the role the immune system plays in the development of type 1 diabetes.
2. What is diabetic ketoacidosis? What causes it?
3. What should a person do if they become hypoglycemic?

Research Projects

Learn more about the discovery of insulin by reading "The Discovery of Insulin" on the website of the Nobel Prize (www.nobelprize. org/educational/medicine/insulin/discovery-insulin.html). What surprises you about this story? Did the scientists make some wrong assumptions?

WORDS TO UNDERSTAND

acanthosis nigricans: a symptom of insulin resistance in which areas of the skin get unusually dark, thick, and velvety.

cardiovascular disease: diseases that affect the heart and blood vessels.

cholesterol: a waxy substance associated with fats that coats the inside of blood vessels, causing cardiovascular disease.

correlation: a connection between different things that suggests they may have something to do with one another.

high blood pressure: when the heart has to use more force than it normally should to pump blood through arteries around the body; also known as hypertension.

metabolic syndrome: a cluster of conditions that occur together, including insulin resistance, obesity, hypertension, and cholesterol problems.

polycystic ovary syndrome (PCOS): an endocrine disorder in girls and women in which the ovaries produce too much of the hormone androgen.

prediabetes: a condition in which blood glucose levels are higher than normal, but not as high as diabetic levels.

prevalence: how common or uncommon a disease is in any given population.

CHAPTER THREE

Type 2 Diabetes

Type 2 diabetes is extremely common in older people. In the United States, one out of every four people ages 65 and older has it. That's 11.8 million elderly people. Type 2 diabetes is much less common among kids. In 2009, researchers estimated that about 5,000 young people between the ages of 10 and 20 had type 2 diabetes. This number sounds small, especially compared to 11.8 million! But not so long ago, most doctors had never even heard of a child or teenager getting type 2 diabetes. The disease was called "adult-onset diabetes" for that reason. Now doctors are very worried about the development of type 2 diabetes in young people.

Type 2 diabetes is a progressive disease that gets worse the longer you have it. As with type 1 diabetes, it has many chronic complications. Heart disease, stroke, kidney disease, blindness, even amputations of the feet and lower legs—all of these problems are common in people who've had diabetes mellitus for a long time. And some of these complications are deadly. The longer you have diabetes, the more likely you are to suffer some of these complications. Doctors are used to seeing these complications in elderly people who developed type 2 diabetes past the age of 40. But since 2001, the **prevalence** of type 2 diabetes in youth has gone up by 30 percent. If current trends continue, it may become common to see chronic complications of type 2 diabetes in much younger people.

Overall, the prevalence of type 2 diabetes in people under 20 is 4.6 out of every 10,000. However, some ethnic groups are more likely to get type 2 diabetes. For both Native American and African American youth, the prevalence of type 2 diabetes is a little over 1 out of every 1,000 kids. For Hispanic and Latino kids, the prevalence is around 8 out of every 10,000 kids.

Young people with type 2 diabetes are usually overweight or obese. They may not get a lot of exercise. They are also more likely to have parents, siblings, or other family members with type 2 diabetes. Often, kids with type 2 diabetes come from homes where families sometimes struggle financially.

A nurse instructs an older lady about how to check her blood sugar levels.

HEART HEALTH AND DIABETES

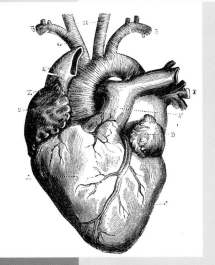

People with diabetes mellitus have a very high risk of developing **cardiovascular disease** over the course of their lifetimes. Cardiovascular disease affects your heart and your blood vessels. The most common type is coronary artery disease. Coronary arteries carry oxygen-filled blood to the heart muscle itself.

Like all muscles, the heart needs oxygen to survive. But fats and **cholesterol** can build up on the inside walls of coronary arteries, making them so narrow that blood has trouble getting through. The heart needs to pump harder to force blood through the narrowed arteries, causing **high blood pressure**. This extra work can damage or weaken the heart, leading to heart failure. A person has a heart attack if a coronary artery gets completely blocked.

Cardiovascular disease is the most common killer of people who've had diabetes for a long time. But if people closely manage their blood glucose levels, they can lower the risk. Keeping to a healthy weight, eating well, and getting regular exercise are also important ways to avoid cardiovascular disease.

They may not always have enough money for healthy foods, and they may not have access to safe spaces for exercising and staying fit. If you have type 2 diabetes, healthy eating and regular exercise are the two most important ways to take care of yourself.

DIABETES
SIGNS AND SYMPTOMS

FREQUENT URINATION

INCREASED THIRST

HUNGER

WEAKNESS

WEIGHT LOSS

BLURRED VISION

NAUSEA

SLOW HEALING OF CUTS/BRUISES

TINGLING IN HANDS

Major symptoms of diabetes.

What Is Type 2 Diabetes?

Type 2 diabetes occurs when cells in the muscles, fat tissue, and liver have trouble using insulin. This is called *insulin resistance*. If insulin is like a key that lets glucose into a cell, insulin resistance is like the sticky lock that doesn't work quite right. Glucose that can't get inside cells builds up in the bloodstream.

Unlike people with type 1 diabetes, people with type 2 diabetes can still make insulin. In fact, the pancreas of a person with type 2 diabetes generally makes *more* insulin, to try to compensate for higher levels of glucose in the bloodstream. But making so much insulin takes a toll on the pancreas. People who have very severe type 2 diabetes, or who have had type 2 diabetes for many years, may eventually find that they lose the ability to make enough insulin to meet their body's needs. They may then require daily injections of insulin.

If you have type 2 diabetes, you may experience many of the same symptoms that someone with type 1 diabetes does. You may feel very tired, or unusually thirsty. You may have to urinate frequently. Your vision might get blurry sometimes, and you might take a long time to get over infections. If you get a cut or a scrape, it might take a long time to heal. If your blood sugar gets very high, you are at risk for the same dangerous acute complications that affect someone with type 1 diabetes, like diabetic ketoacidosis leading to a coma.

But if you have type 2 diabetes or are at high risk for developing it, you may not be aware of it. You may not experience symptoms or feel sick right away. This is why regular check-ups with your pediatrician are so important. It's

EDUCATIONAL VIDEO

Scan this code for a video about living with type 2 diabetes.

FAT: AN ENDOCRINE ORGAN

Doctors have long noted a strong link, or **correlation**, between obesity and certain endocrine disorders, like type 2 diabetes and PCOS. But scientists have only very recently come to realize that fat tissue itself produces endocrine hormones. These are called the *adipokines*. Some, like leptin, affect appetite. Others affect the immune system. And some appear to affect insulin sensitivity. Scientists hope to learn more about how fat functions as an endocrine organ. That will help us understand type 2 diabetes, cardiovascular disease, and many other diseases.

also really important that you take your doctor's recommendations seriously. Insulin resistance may be mild at first. But it gets progressively worse over time. And the earlier you take steps to lower your blood sugar, the better your chances of living a long, healthy life.

Diagnosing Diabetes

How does a doctor determine whether you have insulin resistance? Being overweight or obese is the most important risk factor. If you are overweight or obese, your doctor will be concerned, especially if you have these other, common risk factors:

- One or more family members has type 2 diabetes.
- Your mom had gestational diabetes when she was pregnant with you.
- You belong to a racial or ethnic group with a higher prevalence of type 2 diabetes.

One visible symptom of insulin resistance, called **acanthosis nigricans**, leaves dark, thickened, velvety skin in places where the body creases or bends, like on the neck and under the armpits. Girls with insulin resistance may develop the symptoms of an endocrine disorder known as **polycystic ovary syndrome** (PCOS), including irregular or absent menstrual periods, acne, and increased facial or body hair. PCOS occurs when a woman's ovaries produce too much of the hormone androgen. When there is too much insulin going unused in the body, excess androgens are also produced.

If the presence of the above risk factors and conditions makes your doctor suspect you might have insulin resistance, you will probably have some tests

Some ethnic groups are at greater risk of diabetes than others.

done. Your blood will be tested for two types of cholesterol. High-density lipoprotein (HDL) is good for you; low-density lipoprotein (LDL) is bad for you. If you have low levels of the good kind of cholesterol or high levels of the bad kind, you're at higher risk for type 2 diabetes and cardiovascular disease. You also have a higher risk of type 2 diabetes and cardiovascular disease if you have high blood pressure.

Your doctor may ask to check your fasting blood sugar levels—the amount of glucose still circulating in your blood when you've gone at least eight hours without eating. You may also be checked for your hemoglobin A1C (HbA1C) levels. Also called the HbA1C test, or glycosylated hemoglobin test, this is a blood test that shows how high blood glucose levels have been over the past two to three months. In addition, you may be asked for a urine sample so that your doctor can check your urine for signs of kidney disease.

If your blood glucose levels turn out to be normal, your doctor will probably check them again at least once every three years. If your blood tests reveal that you have mild hyperglycemia, your doctor will talk to you about **prediabetes** or **metabolic syndrome**, depending on the results of your other tests. Both prediabetes and metabolic syndrome put you at very high risk for developing type 2 diabetes.

There are two important lifestyle changes you can make to delay or maybe even prevent yourself from getting type 2 diabetes. Exercise improves the body's ability to use insulin, so your doctor will probably recommend that you exercise regularly. Exercise will also help you develop more muscle and less fat. Fatty tissue produces substances that make it harder for the body to use insulin.

If you're overweight or obese, your doctor will also talk to you about changing your eating habits. To help you control your weight, doctors and nutritionists usually recommend eating smaller portion sizes, fewer animal fats, less sugar, and more fruits and vegetables. These are good ideas for everyone, regardless of whether or not they're at risk for diabetes. Together, you, your family, and your doctor or nutritionist can help you put together a healthy diet

Regular physical activity can help people avoid diabetes.

CARBOHYDRATES

There are three kinds of carbohydrates in food: fiber, complex carbohydrates (also called starches), and sugars. Fiber is an indigestible material produced by plants. It helps digestion, and does not have a big effect on blood glucose.

Potatoes, corn, and beans are complex carbohydrates. So are grains like wheat, oats, and barley, which you'll find in everything from bread and pasta to breakfast cereal. The body breaks complex carbohydrates down to simple sugars, like glucose, for energy. So complex carbohydrates affect your blood sugar.

You also eat sugars directly. Some sugars are added to packaged foods. Other sugars occur naturally in fruit and milk. All types of sugar affect blood glucose.

If you're counting carbs to help control your blood sugar, you should use the "total carbohydrate" number on the nutrition label unless your doctor advises you to do otherwise.

plan that you can stick to. You don't have to keep to your diet perfectly every single day. But when you make good choices about what to eat and how much to exercise, you give your future self the gift of a longer and healthier life.

If your blood tests reveal that your hyperglycemia has already become severe enough to qualify as type 2 diabetes, your doctor may prescribe medication for you, as well as encouraging you to eat a healthy diet and exercise regularly. The most common medication used to treat insulin resistance and type 2 diabetes is called metformin, which is a pill that is usually taken a couple of times per day. Your doctor may prescribe other medications as well. In some cases, you may need to start taking insulin injections, in which case you will need to monitor your daily blood sugar levels, as described in chapter two.

Text-Dependent Questions

1. How has the prevalence of type 2 diabetes changed for kids and teens?
2. What are the risk factors for type 2 diabetes?
3. What are the two important lifestyle changes someone with insulin resistance should make?

Research Projects

The American Diabetes Association (ADA) produces a booklet to help kids and teens with type 2 diabetes. You can read it online at http://main.diabetes.org/dorg/PDFs/Type-2-Diabetes-in-Youth/Type-2-Diabetes-in-Youth.pdf. What are some tips it gives for eating healthily and staying fit? Make a sample menu for yourself of healthy foods to eat over the course of a day.

WORDS TO UNDERSTAND

blood glucose correction factor: the amount by which one unit of insulin lowers blood glucose levels.

glucagon: a hormone made by alpha cells in the islets of Langerhans that increases the amount of glucose in the blood.

insulin-to-carb ratio: the number of grams of carbohydrates that one unit of insulin will cover.

CHAPTER FOUR

Living with Diabetes

If you have diabetes, and especially if you are insulin dependent, your daily routine has a lot of extra steps in it. You get ready for school and eat breakfast, just like every other kid. But first you have to check your blood glucose. You prick your finger with a lancet, place a drop of blood on a test strip, and put the test strip in your blood glucose monitor. The monitor shows you a number. Ideally, it's a number within the range your doctor has recommended for you. If it's low, you might need a snack right away, before you brush your teeth or get dressed. But this snack is just to bring your blood glucose back up. You still need to have breakfast.

What are you having for breakfast? How many grams of carbohydrates does it have? You look at the nutrition label on the package, or maybe you look up the carbohydrate amount in a book or on a website. Now you figure out how much insulin you need to cover the amount of carbs in your breakfast. The **insulin-to-carb ratio** varies from person to person; your doctor and medical team will help you figure yours out. It might be anywhere from 1 unit of insulin for every 8 grams of carbohydrates to 1 unit for every 15 grams. Whatever your personal ratio is, you have to calculate it for the amount of carbs in your breakfast. Then

Managing diabetes starts at breakfast.

you have to adjust that number up or down depending on whether your blood sugar was high or low when you woke up, using the **blood glucose correction factor**. Together, it adds up to your morning insulin dose. Math first thing in the morning? Welcome to life with diabetes.

At School

You probably know the school nurse pretty well. If your school doesn't have a nurse, at least one teacher or administrator has been trained to help you manage your diabetes. Maybe that person gives you your insulin dose before lunch, if you use a syringe and don't give yourself your own shots. Maybe that person has a sharps container to safely dispose of your lancets and syringes. That person is definitely in charge of knowing where your emergency diabetes supplies are.

Younger kids might need help testing their blood sugar at school.

GLUCOSE LEVELS

Blood glucose levels are measured one of two different ways, one for daily readings (milligrams per deciliter, or mg/dl) and one for trends over two to three months (A1C). For both measurements, you have a target range, a goal to keep those values higher than a certain number but lower than another number. Your target range is set by your doctor and medical team according to your individual needs and circumstances. It's generally between 90 and 150–180 mg/dl. Target ranges may be adjusted as you get older, go through puberty, or have other changes in your circumstances.

Some people find it pretty easy to stay within their target range most of the time. Other people find it very hard, no matter how careful they are. That can be really discouraging, but you should never feel like it's your fault. Make sure to keep accurate records of your blood glucose levels. If you're having trouble staying within your target range, your doctor and medical team may be able to adjust your treatment plan to help you out.

He or she knows what to do if you get hyperglycemic or hypoglycemic. An adult trained in diabetes management should be around whenever you're at school or at a school-related activity, just in case.

It's almost lunchtime. Everyone in class gets droopy or fidgety while they wait for lunch, but you're the one who has to do math about it. Even if you have a continuous glucose monitor and an insulin pump, you probably need to do a finger-stick to check your blood glucose levels before lunch. Maybe you go to the nurse's office to do that, but you might do it right in the classroom. After a while, the other kids get used to it and don't notice.

Sometimes they ask you questions, though. It can be kind of a mixed blessing, having everyone know about your diabetes. It's great when your friends can understand and even be helpful about all the extra decisions and tasks you have to do every day. But it can be a pain when kids ask you questions you've heard a million times before. You patiently explain that you can't catch diabetes from someone else, and that you didn't get it from eating too much candy. Sometimes you get tired of doing all the math and answering all the questions. You just want to eat your tuna fish sandwich in peace. But you can't stop being diabetic. You'll always look at your sandwich and mentally calculate that two slices of bread equals 30 grams of carbs.

After school, you have soccer practice. Exercise can really lower your blood sugar, so you always have to be careful to check your blood glucose levels and

Friends might have questions about diabetes.

have glucose-containing snacks or juice on hand in case you need it. You might even disconnect your insulin pump during practice to keep yourself from getting low. But if your coach has you run extra laps today, you might start feeling low anyway. You check your blood glucose levels again. One of your teammates watches you use the lancet on your finger and says, "I could never do that. I hate needles." You just shrug. Nobody loves needles. But you get used to it.

In the Evening

You have to drink some juice and eat two cookies in the car on the way home from soccer, but then you feel fine. If you use an insulin pump, you disconnect it so that you can take a shower. Then you put it back on and do your homework until dinnertime. When your blood sugar is low or high, it can sometimes be hard to concentrate on getting your homework done.

Dinnertime. More math, more insulin. Before bed, you check blood glucose levels again. You don't want your blood glucose to get too high or too

 BASAL/BOLUS

Some people get one long-acting or two intermediate-acting doses of insulin per day. That is basal insulin—it mimics the insulin that a healthy pancreas would supply to the body at all times. That is supplemented with bolus insulin—short-acting doses that mimic the insulin a healthy pancreas would pump into the bloodstream in response to eating. Bolus insulin is generally administered before meals.

A person using an insulin pump gets small doses of short-acting insulin throughout the day as basal insulin. Larger doses before meals act as bolus insulin.

low overnight, but sometimes it happens. Colds, flu, stress, injuries—all these things can make it harder to keep your blood sugar within your healthy range. Sometimes your parents might need to wake you up in the middle of the night to check if you've gotten hyperglycemic or hypoglycemic. If you wear a continuous glucose monitor, it might wake you up with an alarm if you're too high or too low.

EDUCATIONAL VIDEO

Scan this code for a video about the daily life of someone with diabetes.

You think how great it would be if your pump and your glucose monitor could just figure all of this out for you while you slept. You know people are working on making an "artificial pancreas." That's an integrated pump and continuous glucose monitor. If you need more glucose, the pump of the artificial pancreas automatically gives you a dose of **glucagon**, a hormone that tells the body to release stores of glucose. If you need more insulin, it automatically provides that. All day, even while you're sleeping. You think it sounds like a great idea. But until such time as the artificial pancreas is widely available and completely reliable, you're glad that you can stay healthy with the tools that you've got.

Tips for Living with Diabetes

- **Get exercise.** Your doctor will give you advice about how much exercise you should get every day, but it's up to you to figure out what you like to do. Join a soccer team, play pick-up basketball, take a dog for a walk—it's all good as long as you get active.

TRANSPLANTS

For a small percentage of people whose diabetes is very difficult to manage, the solution may be a transplant. That's when an organ from one person's body is surgically placed in another person's body. Type 1 diabetes can be treated with a transplant of the entire pancreas. Doctors are also trying to develop procedures for transplanting just the cells of the islets of Langerhans.

Transplants are very expensive, and there are not enough donated organs for everyone who could use them. Because a body will recognize and attempt to destroy something it identifies as foreign, people who receive transplants have to take very powerful drugs to prevent their immune systems from rejecting the new organ. They may have to take these drugs, which have many side effects, for the rest of their lives. But in some cases, the trade-off is worth it.

- **Get healthy food.** Carrot sticks or potato chips? That's a hard choice the first couple of times you have to make it. But once you get used to choosing food that's good for you, it will become second nature.
- **Get organized.** Make a schedule for your meals and medications. Plan ahead for any special events or activities. Keep track of all your diabetes supplies. Keep a record of your blood glucose levels. Being prepared to meet every day with diabetes will help you learn be prepared for anything.
- **Get to know your body.** Are there situations—like being sick, or stressed, or tired—that make it harder to manage your blood glucose levels? Learn when to look out extra carefully for yourself.
- **Get regular check-ups.** Don't be afraid to talk to your doctor if you have any concerns or questions.

People with diabetes may need to check their blood sugar wherever they are, even if they are eating at a restaurant.

Healthy snacks are an important part of keeping blood sugar under control.

Text-Dependent Questions

1. What are three times during the day when someone with type 1 diabetes has to check blood glucose levels?
2. Explain the difference between basal and bolus insulin.
3. What would an artificial pancreas do?

Research Projects

If you're not insulin dependent, experience what it is like. Play the Diabetic Dog game (available at www.nobelprize.org/educational/medicine/insulin/game/insulin.html) and see how well you can manage the dog's blood glucose levels.

If you are insulin dependent, design your ideal artificial pancreas. What features would it have?

FURTHER READING

American Diabetes Association. "Diabetes Basics." http://www.diabetes.org/diabetes-basics/.

Chaloner, Kim. *Diabetes and Me: An Essential Guide for Kids and Their Parents.* New York: Hill and Wang, 2013.

Children with Diabetes. http://www.childrenwithdiabetes.com/.

Diapedia: The Living Textbook of Diabetes. http://www.diapedia.org/.

Drum, David, and Terry Zierenberg. *The Type 2 Diabetes Sourcebook.* New York: McGraw-Hill, 2006.

Lawton, Sandra Augustyn, ed. *Diabetes Information for Teens: Health Tips about Managing Diabetes and Preventing Related Complications, Including Facts about Insulin, Glucose Control, Healthy Eating, Physical Activity, and Learning to Live with Diabetes.* Detroit, MI: Omnigraphics, 2006.

Loy, Spike, and Bo Loy. *Getting a Grip on Diabetes: Quick Tips and Techniques for Kids and Teens.* Alexandria, VA: American Diabetes Association, 2007.

Educational Videos

Chapter One: KidsHealth.org. "How the Endocrine System Works." https://www.youtube.com/watch?v=HXPCQBD_WGI.

Chapter Two: SophiaType1D. "What's in My Bag?" https://www.youtube.com/watch?v=O288S_DxTwc.

Chapter Three: KidsHealth.org "Diabetes: DJ's Story." https://www.youtube.com/watch?v=ss5W-Wz-RTo.

Chapter Four: The Diabetes Site. "A Day in the Life of Type One Diabetes." http://blog.thediabetessite.com/a-day-in-the-life-of-type-1-diabetes/.

SERIES GLOSSARY

accommodation: an arrangement or adjustment to a new situation; for example, schools make accommodations to help students cope with illness.

anemia: an illness caused by a lack of red blood cells.

autoimmune: type of disorder where the body's immune system attacks the body's tissues instead of germs.

benign: not harmful.

biofeedback: a technique used to teach someone how to control some bodily functions.

capillaries: tiny blood vessels that carry blood from larger blood vessels to body tissues.

carcinogens: substances that can cause cancer to develop.

cerebellum: the back part of the brain; it controls movement.

cerebrum: the front part of the brain; it controls many higher-level thinking and functions.

cholesterol: a waxy substance associated with fats that coats the inside of blood vessels, causing cardiovascular disease.

cognitive: related to conscious mental activities, such as learning and thinking.

communicable: transferable from one person to another.

congenital: a condition or disorder that exists from birth.

correlation: a connection between different things that suggests they may have something to do with one another.

dominant: in genetics, a dominant trait is expressed in a child even when the trait is only inherited from one parent.

environmental factors: anything that affects how people live, develop, or grow. Climate, diet, and pollution are examples.

genes: units of hereditary information.

hemorrhage: bleeding from a broken blood vessel.

hormones: substances the body produces to instruct cells and tissues to perform certain actions.

inflammation: redness, swelling, and tenderness in a part of the body in response to infection or injury.

insulin: a hormone produced in the pancreas that controls cells' ability to absorb glucose.

lymphatic system: part of the human immune system; transports white blood cells around the body.

malignant: harmful; relating to tumors, likely to spread.

mutation: a change in the structure of a gene; some mutations are harmless, but others may cause disease.

neurological: relating to the nervous system (including the brain and spinal cord).

neurons: specialized cells found in the central nervous system (the brain and spinal cord).

occupational therapy: a type of therapy that teaches one how to accomplish tasks and activities in daily life.

oncology: the study of cancer.

orthopedic: dealing with deformities in bones or muscles.

prevalence: how common or uncommon a disease is in any given population.

prognosis: the forecast for the course of a disease that predicts whether a person with the disease will get sicker, recover, or stay the same.

progressive disease: a disease that generally gets worse as time goes on.

psychomotor: relating to movement or muscle activity resulting from mental activity.

recessive: in genetics, a recessive trait will only be expressed if a child inherits it from both parents.

remission: an improvement in or disappearance of someone's symptoms of disease; unlike a cure, remission is usually temporary.

resilience: the ability to bounce back from difficult situations.

seizure: an event caused by unusual brain activity resulting in physical or behavior changes.

syndrome: a condition with a set of associated symptoms.

ulcers: a break or sore in skin or tissue where cells disintegrate and die. Infections may occur at the site of an ulcer.

INDEX

Illlustrations are indicated by page numbers in *italic* type.

ABOUT THE ADVISOR

Heather Pelletier, Ph.D., is a pediatric staff psychologist at Rhode Island Hospital/ Hasbro Children's Hospital with a joint appointment as a clinical assistant professor in the departments of Psychiatry and Human Behavior and Pediatrics at the Warren Alpert Medical School of Brown University. She is also the director of behavioral pain medicine in the division of Children's Integrative therapies, Pain management and Supportive care (CHIPS) in the department of Pediatrics at Hasbro Children's Hospital. Dr. Pelletier provides clinical services to children in various medical specialty clinics at Hasbro Children's Hospital, including the pediatric gastroenterology, nutrition, and liver disease clinics.

ABOUT THE AUTHOR

Rebecca Sherman writes about health care policy, public health issues, and parenting. She lives in Massachusetts with her family.

PHOTO CREDITS

Cover: iStock/Fertnig

iStock: 10 robertprzybysz ; 24 Fertnig; 27 Irina Strelnikova; 28 Fertnig; 31 MarkHatfield; 36 AlexRaths; 37 ilbusca; 38 Irina Strelnikova; 41 vgajic; 43 FatCamera; 44 robynmac; 48 kajakiki; 49 Fertnig; 51 kali9; 55 vgajic; 56 HandmadePictures

Shutterstock 12 marina_ua; 13 Designua; 16 Image Point Fr; 19 Designua

Wellcome Images: 20; 26; 29

Wikimedia: 32 Official White House Photostream